1066

AND ALL THAT

1916

AND ALL THAT

A HISTORY OF
IRELAND
FROM BACK THEN
UNTIL RIGHT NOW

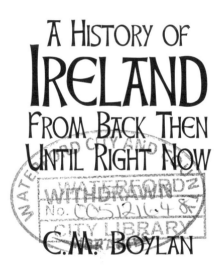

C.M. BOYLAN

The
History
Press
Ireland

First published 2012

The History Press Ireland
50 Quay Street
Dublin 2
Ireland
www.thehistorypress.ie

British Library Cataloguing in Publication Data.
A catalogue record for this book is available from the British Library.

ISBN 978 1 84588 749 0

Typesetting and origination by The History Press

CONTENTS

SHORT INTRODUCTION

The word 'historiography' can be defined as all the accumulated writings on a topic of history. The historiography of Henry VIII's reign, for instance, is all the books and articles that have been written about Henry VIII's time as king. This body of work will include any number of controversies and disagreements between scholars of Henry VIII as to what he said, what he did, what he meant by what he said, what he meant to say he did and what he said he meant to do.

I mention historiography, firstly, and most importantly, to sound intelligent. I mention historiography, secondly, and quite importantly, to explain that I will not be drawing upon the historiography of Irish historical happenings. This is because this is not an 'academic history'. Academic histories habitually make use of historiography, which they like to point out in footnotes. Footnotes are references to the work of other historians whose writings you are 'citing', 'drawing upon', 'employing to enhance your own argument' or 'stealing'.

This is an example of an academic footnote.[1] Aside from ignoring the historiography and excluding footnotes, there is one other way in which this book differentiates itself from academic history: its wholesale neglect of what are commonly called 'facts'. These are considered important by academic historians, who spend minutes and even hours looking for them in old letters, manuscripts, diaries, books and Google. In this account, where any facts appear, they occupy the status of happy accidents or nice surprises.

The Irish have been noted for their obsession with their own history. Some say the Irish are obsessed with their history because they have had such a bad one; others because the Irish mind inclines towards narrative; others still because as islanders we are naturally insular and vain. I won't be drawn on this topic, but I'm sure you have your own opinion on the matter. Which brings me to one final point in this short introduction: if I unintentionally express any 'opinion' in this history, it is, just like the joyous coincidence that I may recount any facts, an inadvertent accident.

I sincerely hope that, like most history books, this one helps you to understand fleetingly and forget instantly everything that you read.

C.M. Boylan, 2012

---

1   For a detailed account of this argument see Sellars & Yeatman *et. al.*, *op. cit, 1066 & All That* (London: Methuen, 1930) 812th edition, *ibid.*, pp 1-1,003.

1

SETTLING EARLY

Irish history started when people arrived on the island. At least, that is when history really got going. Before that things were rather quiet: mountains rose groaning from the ground, rivers carved long, deep valleys, and trees peacefully spread their roots and branches. The first people, or 'earliest settlers' as they are sometimes known, came from Continental Europe to disturb this calm. They were Stone Age people, so named because they adored stone. They made everything from stone – or 'flint' as it was known at the time – even their shoes and clothes. As a result, they rarely had good posture.

These earliest settlers arrived a very long time ago, before the wheel was invented and long, long before pillowcases. Eventually, they began to farm, which was much less taxing than spearing berries and gathering boar, and they settled into communities.

Aside from farming, their favourite activity was building tombs; in particular, megalithic tombs such as court cairns, portal dolmens and passage tombs. These were often large, impressive and, perhaps unsurprisingly, stone based. Tomb-building was nothing short of a mania and eventually the tombs vastly outnumbered the amount of available dead. It was therefore agreed to bury much-loved household pets in the superfluous tombs, leading to entire portal dolmens housing the bones of a single ungrateful cat.

The most famous of all ancient Irish tombs is the narrow passage tomb at Newgrange in County Meath, which proves beyond doubt that claustrophobia did not exist in 3200 BC but is an entirely modern ailment. About 200,000 tonnes of stone were used during the construction of Newgrange, begging the question: what were they thinking?

Note:
Historians often begin with questions such as this one, which they use to guide their research. For instance, nobody would know anything about the Battle of Waterloo unless one inspired historian had asked, 'Where did Napoleon go that week?' It turned out that he had gone to battle, at Waterloo.

The people at this time drew spiral decorations on every available surface from stones to rocks and boulders. Historians are deeply divided over whether this represented a primitive attempt to hypnotise one another or a simple love of twirling. This is called a 'historical debate'.

One final point to be noted about these early settlers is that they appear to have worshipped the otter as some form of god or emperor, as evidenced by the many forty-foot statues of otters that have been unearthed across the country dating from this period, most of which depict the otter standing upright on its hind legs, looking magisterial.

Test Your Knowledge:
1. In this stone-based economy, how many pebbles did a pebble necklace cost?

2. What is a historical debate and who won?

3. Why was stone called 'flint' and not some other word?

2

THIRD BEST METAL

People in Europe eventually discovered how to mine for metal and make infinitely sturdier weapons and tools than the granite axes and limestone screwdrivers they had previously employed. After a while they created a metal called bronze. This was the third best metal ever made, but it was still quite effective. The next age, therefore, was the Bronze Age.

Eventually, some Bronze Age people moved to Ireland. Ireland's early metalworkers were also called the 'Beaker' people because they evidently enjoyed conducting science experiments. Laboratory after laboratory has been unearthed by archaeologists all over Ireland, littered with countless numbers of beakers, pipettes and primitive Bunsen burners. Quite what these experiments were aimed at is unclear, as precious few hardback science copybooks were found amongst the remains of these ancient labs.

The further back in time one goes, the more difficult it is for historians to reconstruct a detailed picture of the society at the time. This is down to a lack of remaining sources from the past. Professor Gonigle McGonigle of a university explains:

It is very difficult to 'converse' with the past at a great distance, to ask it questions or receive any clear replies. It is the equivalent of having an exasperating afternoon sandwich with a drunken Dutchman – only snippets of sense can be gleaned.

You might therefore assume that history books about the distant past would be shorter. You would be wrong. This is because in the absence of source-based facts, historians instead proffer fanciful conjectures on how things might have been. That a great many works on early history lapse into fantasy novels featuring dragons and magic trees is one unfortunate upshot of this historiographical travesty.

While these Bronze Agers made many progressive strides in metallurgy and state science exams, our knowledge of their lives is still rather hazy. We do know that they made lovely pottery and jewellery. From this we might postulate that they were very house-proud and glamorous.

Indeed, jewellery-making replaced tomb-building as the main activity, to the extent that the only tombs that were invented during this period were wedge tombs, a comparatively perfunctory form of burial house when compared with its impressive funerary predecessors. The jewellery, by contrast,

was exquisite and of such variety – from earrings to bracelets and leg ornaments – that it is very likely that people dressed entirely in jewellery rather than clothes.

Although bronze was a very good metal, it was, as noted, not quite the best. Some people in Europe therefore invented an even stronger and more durable metal called iron, with which to make axes, swords and cheese graters. The next age, therefore, was the Iron Age.

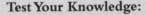

Test Your Knowledge:
1. To what extent was the above: (a) true, (b) lovely, (c) above?

3

Fiery, Warlike

The Celts were a group of Iron Agers who originated in Central Europe. Being a fiery and warlike people, they conquered much of that continent before arriving in Ireland. Historians are still undecided as to exactly how the Celts arrived and from where, but the most likely scenario is that they flew here on giant eagles from Biarritz around 600 BC.

The Celts of Celtic Ireland created a complex society that deserves to be described under headings.

Celtic Dwellings

The Celts lived in various types of fortified enclosures of mottled daub, which they then daubed with more mottle. There were ringforts, which were round; hill forts, which were round and on hills; and crannógs, which were round and in lakes. Inside the ringforts, hill forts and crannógs the Celts ate, slept and made Tara brooches. Brooch after brooch after handcrafted brooch was produced by the eager jewellers, until eventually they became as commonplace and worthless as gravel. People took to throwing down a layer of brooches on their driveways or flinging excess brooches onto roads and pathways with a bored insouciance that would shock modern sensibilities. This made visiting neighbours or simply going for a casual stroll a treacherous affair, and cases of 'brooch foot' are numerously described in the annals.

Celtic Society I: Hierarchy

The country was divided into kingdoms called 'tuatha', each of which was ruled by a chieftain. Other types of people also existed. Here is a table to help you understand what each of these people did:

Name	What they would be today
Druid	Priest
Brehon	Judge
File	Poet
Freeman	Rich person
Unfree man	Poor person

Celtic society was very hierarchical. This is a difficult word to pronounce, but it is important as it refers to the very complex sociological issue of who was better than who in every way. The chieftains were better than the druids, brehons and filí; the druids, brehons and filí were better than the freemen, and the freemen were better than the unfree men, who could not own property or carry weapons. The cow occupied a respectable middle ground between freemen and filí. Sheep, by contrast, were considered as lowly as unfree men, and were sometimes bullied openly for their lack of sophistication and learning. The plight of the Celtic sheep is just one of the many overlooked areas of Irish history.

Learning Exercise:
Imagine you are a Celtic sheep. How would you feel and when would you feel it? Is it fair that you are not a cow? What would be your favourite colour?

Celtic Society II: War

Being famously fiery and warlike, the Celts battled each other on a near-constant basis. Sometimes the Celts went on cattle raids, stealing cow after respectable cow (see above). More often, they went to war with rival clans, fighting in chariots with swords, shields, slings and javelins. They were very much like pale Romans in this respect.

The most famous male warrior was Cúchulainn. He also invented hurling and had a dog called Santa, proving conclusively that Christmas existed well before Christ.

Celtic Society III: Dreamy, Merry

As well as being fiery and warlike, the Celts were also dreamy and merry, as this vivid and moving account from the epic saga *Cúl Mac Cúl agus an Bó Mór Iontach* illustrates:

> And lo, on a dreamy night we made merry and feasted heavily inside our fortified fort of daubed mottle, etc.

Meat at such feasts was cooked on a fulacht fiadh, which was very like a modern-day microwave but with fire, stones and water in place of high-frequency electromagnetic waves.

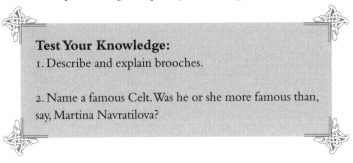

Test Your Knowledge:

1. Describe and explain brooches.

2. Name a famous Celt. Was he or she more famous than, say, Martina Navratilova?

4

SHAMROCKS

Before Christianity arrived Ireland was pagan, which was a bad thing because nobody knew about sin or heaven or purgatory or Mass, all of which are good things to know about in case they start happening to you. The person who brought Christianity to Ireland was St Patrick, a young shepherd from Wales who was kidnapped and brought to Ireland, this being the main form of job recruitment at the time.

Patrick spent many years trying to explain the complex concept of the Holy Trinity to the eager simpletons of Ireland. He drew Venn diagrams, made papier-mâché God heads and wrote endless limericks to explain the idea, but it was only when he plucked a shamrock from the ground in complete plucking exasperation that everybody finally got it.

The people praised St Patrick with a parade and drunken binge.

Learning Exercise:
Imagine you are an important Christian sent to convert some heathens. How would you explain 'transubstantiation' using only the following aids: a plank of wood, a tulip, a tear on a child's face?

Two other important early Irish Christians were St Bridget, who invented the first day of Spring, and St Colmcille, who invented Irish monks. Ireland was known as the land of saints and scholars, and historians have estimated that 3.5 out of every 4 Irish people were monks at this time. As a result, there was a huge import trade in sackcloth, vellum and anti-toupees (bald-head coverings for resolutely hirsute people unable to maintain a tonsure).

The monks founded monasteries in the most remote and isolated parts of the country they could find. One such place was Sceilig Mhichíl, a treacherous rocky outcrop in the wild Atlantic that up until this point had been populated by puffins, who reigned there in lordly dominion. The famous Battle of the Puffins, during which the monks fought for space to build their monastery, is described in the *Annals of the Four Puffins*, from the eighth century:

> The great battle commenced with the puffins wheeling and diving at the beleaguered monks who wanted nothing but a treacherous rocky outcrop upon which to pray and shave their heads. After eight days and two nights of the most violent pecking and squawking, peace descended and the two – monk and puffin – have shared the holy crag ever since, thanks be to Shamrock.

How the battle is recounted in puffin history is not known, as puffins are famously illiterate.

Monks were fiercely competitive in their search for the most isolated monastic site, leading one monk – St Fintubar – to found a monastery under the sea. Due to his inability to breathe in his briny priory, he abandoned his plan and settled instead on a basalt projection thirty miles off the coast of Antrim.

Monks lived famously disciplined lives following the Rule of St Benedict, which said:

Monks must rise at 1 a.m. (11 p.m. in summer) and must not yawn or rub their eyes.

Monks must not eat more than two daily meals in the refectory, neither of which is to contain more than three tastes.

Monks must attend church to chant at the following: matins, vespers, elevenses, lauds, lullabies.

Praying must be undertaken audibly enough for a mouse to be alarmed but not so audibly as to scare a jumpy nun.

Flagellation must be self-inflected and vigorous.

Irish monks spread far and wide across Europe, e.g. Bobbio, Lindisfarne. This was our first time abroad and we made a very good impression – an achievement subsequent generations have been enthusiastically undoing. Overall, though, this was a very pious period of our history and therefore somewhat boring.

5

Vikings and High Kings

The pious tedium of the period was broken by waves of invasions by Scandinavians in helmets, known as 'Vikings' or 'Norsemen'. The Vikings were a fiery and warlike people who built impressive long ships called longships, established impressive long ports called longphorts, and travelled about ransacking, pillaging and plundering to great effect.

The Vikings, being most at home on the sea, plundered primarily along the coast and they rarely made it further inland than a seagull on day out. Indeed, it has been surmised that they may have suffered from a congenital inability to cope with inland regions. One account left by Henrik the Helmeted depicted what would nowadays be diagnosed as a full-blown panic attack, when he found himself deep in present-day Louth:

> The land was dry and sealess for miles around and my heart began
> to pound louder and louder. I screamed out to Thor for a gull or
> a tern, but nothing, nothing but hills, grass and ground which did

not move up and down but remained terrifyingly solid. At last I
came upon a rivulet and threw my face into it to feel its watery
comfort. At this point, I passed out.

Account of the Plundering of Future-Day Louth, AD 912.

The Vikings plundered
monasteries for their stores
of wealth, so the monks
attempted to protect themselves and their treasures by
building Round Towers.
One monk was chosen to
guard the treasure, his job
being to live at the top of
the tower and grow his
hair. He was known as the
'Rapunzel Monk', and
when an invading band
of Vikings was spotted,
the Rapunzel Monk
would drop his hair to
the ground to allow his
fellow ecclesiastics to
clamber to safety.

Some Vikings found the near-incessant pillaging and ransacking tiring, and so decided to relax and stay in Ireland, inventing towns such as Waterford, which means 'Ford of water' in Norse, and Limerick, which comes from the Norse words for sea (*limer*) and gull (*icke*). The Vikings were also the first to introduce money to Ireland, which baffled everybody until it was explained using a shamrock. They likewise brought fjords, carving one in Connemara called Killary Harbour sometime around the year 850. So strong were the mighty Vikings that Killary was carved by only three men – Thorin, Bjornin and Klorin – using nothing but two chisels and a rusty hammer. Interestingly, the county of Longford is named after this long fjord, despite its being well over seventy miles away. This was done in an attempt to give Longford some historical meaning.

Over time, the Vikings grew in strength and they eventually controlled a small kingdom stretching from Skerries to Arklow, which historians have agreed are the most underwhelming perimeters of a kingdom ever recorded.

Since the Vikings were fiery and warlike, and since they had settled in a country of fiery and warlike people, it was only a matter of time before a substantial ruckus took place. This was the Battle of Clontarf, between the High King Brian Boru and approximately 800,000 Vikings. Brian won easily with the help of a magic tree, but while in his tent, praying to a shamrock, he was murdered by a cowardly retreating Viking.

The battle signalled the end of Viking power in Dublin. From then on the Vikings decided it would be easier to convert to Christianity, learn Irish, marry natives and wear brooches. This is called 'assimilation'. It was a trend that caught on with future invader-settlers or 'invado-settlers'.

Test Your Knowledge:

1. Complete the following sentence: The Vikings were
_____, _____, and twelve _____ their _____
sometimes.

2. Was Brian Boru a High King, a Viking, a wedding ring
or a flower in spring?

3. How much is money worth?

6

ANGLO-NORMANS

The next wave of invado-settlers was the Anglo-Normans, whom historians have often described as fiery and warlike.

The first part of the Anglo-Norman invasion of Ireland was in fact not an invasion at all. A Norman knight called Strongbow was invited to Ireland by Dermot MacMurrough, the deposed King of Leinster, who needed help to win his kingdom back. Strongbow was so called because of the impressive strength of his bow. Almost all the Irish nobility he had bowed before remarked on the flexibility and lowness of his bow, the strength of which was concentrated in his genetically overlarge calves, which are, obviously, the main bowing muscle.

Henry II, the Anglo-Norman King of England, became jealous of these showy bow-ey antics and invaded Ireland to put Strongbow in his place, after which he decreed himself Lord of Ireland and Duchess of Cavan in a grand ceremony.

Revisionist Note #1:
Some people take the invasion of Henry II to mark the beginning of 800 years of Irish oppression at the hands of the English. In fact, it was 751 years of oppression which has been rounded up to suit the interests of those who prize zeros and slogans over history and truth.

The Normans continued to conquer large areas of Ireland and went around building castles made of mottes, moats, keeps and baileys to defend against those who were 'mere Irish'. These structures dotted the landscape and indeed historians estimate that 5.8 out of every 7.2 people in Ireland lived within roaring distance of a castle.

Another thing the Normans liked to build was defensive walls, mainly around towns but also around shrubs, livestock, children and other walls. Wall after sturdy wall has been uncovered in archaeological excavations across the country. It is estimated that between 1200 and 1450, as much as 58 per cent of available land was covered by some form of wall.

Given the amount of time they spent building walls, the Normans were understandably fiercely proud of their masonry, and often suffered from severe wall envy when visiting other towns. This is an account of a visit by Henry Fitzbutler de Bourke, Mayor of Athenry, to the town of Drogheda:

> The walls of Drogheda town are stronge and thicke as an oxen's hide. This vexes me to madness! I have determined that the walls of Athenry be increased by twenty-four widths of wall 'til it takes a man half a day's riding to pass throughe the very walls.

walled castle

walled village

walled wood

walled tree

walled wall

walled wall-eyed sheep

Furthermore to this, I shalle build a scale model of the new wall on the display wall in the market square (note possibility of renaming market square 'Wall Square'). The townspeople here are uniformly foule to beholde and their stench is of cabbage.

Test Your Knowledge:
1. Why were walls the be wall and end wall for the Normans?

7

TU DOR OR NOT TU DOR

n July 1504, there were three types of area in Ireland – the Pale, the lands of the Anglo-Norman lords, and the lands of the Gaelic lords – defined by their ever-diminishing levels of Englishness. Thus, people in the Pale were extremely English (custard, radio plays, cricket matches, etc.) while the population of the Gaelic lands were extremely un-English (no custard, no radio plays, no cricket matches, etc.). The Anglo-Normans, in an extended (and, some historians maintain, self-imposed) bout of senility had forgotten most of their Englishness and were therefore called the 'Old English'.

England's most famous ever king, Henry VIII, decided that he would like to conquer Ireland fully and entirely, and make it wholly English. Henry was a Tudor and is therefore sometimes known as Henry Tudor, or 'Hendor' for short. Hendor found a convenient excuse for his Irish conquest in the shape of 'Silken Thomas', son of the powerful Earl of Kildare. Thomas was a troubled young man with an ostentatious addiction to silk and silken products. When he heard that Henry

intended to increase import duties on silk, he jumped straight
on his horse in a pair of jodhpurs (silk) and rode to London
to demand the duties be revoked instantly. Henry had a great
matter at the time and so refused to deal with him, whereupon
Thomas flung down his sword and called him a 'total b★★★★'.
An angry Hendor immediately sent an army to Ireland, where
he crushed the mighty Fitzgeralds and took their large estates.

Hendor, being greedy for more Irish land and realising war was an expensive means of acquiring this, came up with an ingenious policy called 'Surrender and Re-pant'. Under this plan, the Gaelic chieftains would surrender their pants in a grand de-panting ceremony. The pants would then be 're-panted' to them, as long as they promised to become his loyal subjects and follow English customs. This worked very well, as it played on the Gaelic chieftains' debilitating weakness for lavish ceremonies and taking off their pants.

The Gaelic chieftains were given English titles and allowed to sit in Parliament. Thus Mac Fionnrua Óg O'Domhnaill became Dame Alabaster O'Donnell, while Maeliascaigh Mór Beag Bán O'Neill became Viceroy Archibald Cotswold.

Learning Exercise:
Imagine you were re-panted and given a title. What would that title be? You may choose from the following: Archbishop, Baroness, Heir-apparent.

The Gaelic chieftains, however, were somewhat slippery in their promises, and before long were back attacking the Pale and generally being as Irish as the Irish themselves.

8

GARDENING

A new scheme for conquering Ireland was by now badly needed. It was decided by a (slightly drunk) Queen Mary Tudor that English and Scottish people should be planted in the soils of Ireland, there to grow and flourish and spread their seeds in the wind. She travelled to Laois and Offaly, where she planted Englishmen and women into the soil and waited until spring for them to sprout. Sadly for Mary (by now very drunk), the anticipated blossoming of gardens of Englishness did not take place. Indeed, as a result her folly, several of these English 'plants' developed severe, and understandable, phobias of mulching and pruning.

Mary decided instead to settle people onto native Irish lands where they could roam free and rule, though the horticultural terminology remained in use when describing the scheme. Lord St Tuffington de Cloud, the Chief Deputy Privy Officer, explained some of the rules that applied to the new plants:

Settler plants are not to mix with the native weeds, rent land to them or marry their admittedly very attractive daughters. They are to sow the seeds of Englishness and weed out any Irishness, creating a compost heap of hope as they go.

The first plantation was not a success, owing to the propensity for the settlers to be raided by Gaelic clans. They determined to do it better next time.

Revisionist Note #2:

Historians have for many years vigorously debated whether Ireland was ever truly 'colonised' or a 'colony'. There is much to consider as part of this complex debate. As one possibly eminent historian has put it:

The literal definition of colonisation … and as such therefore … kingdom of settlement! … evident empire-builders … what? … geographico-economic assimilation of the socio-historical nexus of connections … the 'cream bun' symbolism of the revisionist movement … quasi … a post-colonial pudding of shame. Edward Said.

How the Irish Became Subaltern Slave Women: Ireland 1500-July 1852
(1998).

As this makes clear, one side is quite obviously right.

The next attempt at gardening was the Munster Plantation. This was organised by Queen Elizabeth I, Henry's other, more famous daughter. Huge English gardens were planted. Sir Walter Raleigh, who invented the potato, the bicycle and the roast potato, was himself planted on 42,000 acres. This effort was much more successful, with four croquet teams forming a Munster League in 1593 and Thurles opening a branch of Barclay's Bank in 1598.

In Ulster, the Gaelic way of life (wolfhounds, bards, etc.) continued to prevail under the last two great Gaelic chieftains, O'Neill and O'Donnell. They decided to lead a rebellion against Elizabeth, which became the Nine Years' War, lasting approximately nine years. The final great battle was the Battle of Kinsale, in which the English defeated everyone including some Spaniards, who had shown up for no reason. The two chieftains were forced to sign a treaty which said they could keep their lands but they had to give up Gaelic customs, which is a bit like giving somebody a car without a steering wheel.

All of this harrowing misfortune for the Irish brought about the Flight of the Girls, during which hundreds of Gaelic girls set sail for France, rather than stay in Ireland and be forced to read the Book of Common Prayer and butter crumpets day after day.

The Plantation of Ulster came next and was very successful, leading to Presbyterians and diamond-shaped marketplaces. The English then sent Oliver Cromwell to Ireland to finish this extensive gardening job. The Cromwellian Plantation sent any remaining Catholic landowners to hell or Clonmel – a bleak land of windswept rocks and miserable craggy shrubs, where no sane person would want to eke out an existence. It is curious that in England Cromwell is remembered as a heroic champion of democracy while in Ireland he is remembered as a Celt-killing religious lunatic. It is likely that the truth lies somewhere in between and that he was, in fact, a heroic champion of religious lunacy.

Thus, after centuries of Irish Catholics owning most of the country, Protestant settlers now controlled almost everything.

Test Your Knowledge:
1. Give the five main characteristics of an acre of land.

9

WILLIAM FIGHT WAR

Soon after these events, considerably more history took place in the shape of the battles between Kings William and James. This was the 'William Fight War', so named because William fought wars. This was actually a bit of English history that spilled over into Ireland because too much history was taking place over there, what with Charles II, *habeas corpus*, old pretenders, Isaac Newton, etc. It was also a bit of European history that was blown over to Ireland by Louis IV. This is important to note, as it reminds us that not all Irish history was made in Ireland (see Appendix B).

The background is complicated and therefore will be largely ignored, but it involved the Glorious deposing of James II (who was also James VII, Harold VI and Angela VIII, due to a coronation oversight) as King of the three Kingdoms by King William, who was his son-in-law and therefore disrespectful. James was a Stuart and so his supporters were called Jacobites. He had been in exile for many years on an orange-tree plantation in Spain, which is why William is often called William of

Orange. James was determined to win back his many thrones and found support amongst Irish people (mainly, it must be said, Catholics), who thought that if Irish history climbed onto the back of English history while riding the wave of European history, they might win back power.

Thus followed the Battle of the Boyne and the Battle of Aughrim, both of which James lost on behalf of Ireland. This episode brought the practice of allowing Englishmen onto Ireland's team into disrepute for centuries, until the era of Italia '90, when the practice was broadly reinstated as a great thing.

The Treaty of Limerick, which ended the wars, forbade Catholics from recognising James as anything other than a mad-haired fool and banished all the wild geese to France. The tame geese were allowed to remain, as they were the lynchpins of domestic service in Ireland at the time, making up 68 per cent of the country's parlour maids.

Following this series of events, Gaelic Ireland was lost forever, like withered gorse on the mountainside, leading to a deluge of poetry and lament.

Translation of 'Oíche na géanna brónach' by Caora Rua Ó Mhíchílín (1715)

Wherefore go the sad geese on the shivering tide?
What is the moonless night that shakes the nest of the crow?
The sons of the Gael are lost tonight!

The poets are starving on the side of the road,
The priests and warriors are definitely sad,
The noble blood is cold in the veins of the high born cattle.

Come, sweet Éireann and suckle your sons!
With your hair of shining gold and your golden belt and shoes,
Reawaken the valour in the bloodied hoof of the first born calf of Fionn!

Test Your Knowledge:
1. Why did history not stay in England and what does this tell us about the size of history?

2. Describe and explain Limerick.

10

PROTESTANTS ASCENDING

Even though the Protestants had won the recent wars, they still felt as insecure as a teenage girl at a party and therefore sought to further undermine Catholic power to make themselves feel thinner and prettier. The Penal Laws were very harsh anti-Catholic laws that aimed at destroying the influence of Catholics in society. Here are the main Penal Laws:

- Catholics may not own property, make money or advance in society.
- Catholics may not sit in Parliament or hold high public office.
- Catholics may not wear nice pyjamas but only ones made of itchy wool.
- Catholics may not turn left but must turn right and then wheel around and head straight.
- Catholics may not call their pets Catholic names such as Holy Mary the dog or Mellifont the cat, but must call their pets Protestant names such as Reginald or Sandwich. The same law applies to children.

- Catholics must always part their hair in the centre, even when it doesn't suit their face.

As some historians have noted, not all of the Penal Laws were rigidly enforced. For instance, the law banning Catholics from turning left aimed to delay Catholics on the way to Mass. However, as Mass was banned this law was not strictly enforced and most Catholics continued to turn left. Most Catholics also continued to attend Mass.

Historians have referred to this period as the 'Protestant Ascendancy', due to the large number of Protestants ascending the ladder of economic and social privilege to the roof of domination. Protestants had most of the land, most of the money and over 94 per cent of cravats. Many Protestants lived in big houses on vast estates called 'demesnes' (pronounced 'land–ed–es–tates').

This was a wonderful time to be alive if you were a Protestant in Ireland. You would have had your own parliament, where you would have decided how velvet your breeches should be. You would have been driven around your sprawling country manor in a gilded carriage, eating truffles and cake, before gathering each evening around your harpsichord to sing songs such as the popular ''Tis grand to be a Protestant Landlord'. Then you would have been an absentee in London for the season, taking multiple turns about the room.

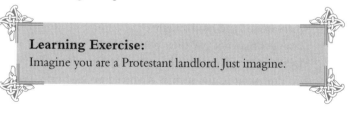

Learning Exercise:
Imagine you are a Protestant landlord. Just imagine.

If you were Catholic at this time, you would have lived in a mud hut with two pigs and seventeen children, and a tiny plot of land consisting of at least 53 per cent rock. You would have dressed in rags with gouged-out turnips for shoes and eaten a diet comprising potatoes or potato substitute (turnip). If your parents could afford it, you would have received schooling underneath a thorny hedge, and every single day you would have attended Mass (with a long sermon) in a barn.

One English visitor to Ireland at the time left the following diary entry:

County Tipperary, 1785. In the morning I visited a local tenant family who lived in a squalid mud hut. When I knocked upon the door a pig answered and snorted in the direction of the woman of the house, who introduced herself as 'Poor Aul' Maggie'. She explained that twelve of her twenty-three children were out ploughing the field, whilst the rest were playing a game of 'stack the potatoes on the pig'. They looked happy enough, if utterly filthy. When I brought this up with Viscount Richacre at supper that evening, he simply scoffed an orange and asked what he might possibly do. He said he gave them a Bible and a telling off four years ago but it had little effect. One does wonder what ought to be done. Nightgown itchy again tonight.

At this time Dublin was a fine, handsome and splendid city. It is hard to imagine now, as you sit along the quays watching a rubbish truck empty its contents on top of a child who continues his stand-off with a pigeon over a half-eaten sandwich, but Dublin at this time was compared to Paris ('the Paris of Ireland') and Bruges ('the Venice of the North, of Ireland'), such was its singular beauty and grand charm.

Ireland had its own parliament of Protestants at the time, and some did look for reform. They felt that the Irish Parliament had too little power compared to the Parliament in London, like a child whose mother lets it make 'beep beep' sounds when she toots the horn. One such peeved Protestant, Henry Grattan, did set up a parliament in his living room with a few Volunteers, and they passed some laws on the cost of port without asking the King, but on the whole this wasn't a huge step forward.

Learning Exercise:
1. Make a list of history so far. Why did it happen in that particular order? Which is your third favourite bit? Is it leading anywhere?

11

IRISHMEN UNITED

Lots of Irish people were unhappy with the situation at the time. They wanted to topple the ascendancy from the rooftop of domination and send them tumbling to the muddy ground of democratic republicanism. They joined together to form the Society of the United Irishmen Against the Situation at This Time, or United Irishmen for short.

The most famous United Irishman was Theobald Wolfe Tone, Ireland's best ever revolutionary, with arguably the greatest name in Irish history. Wolfe Tone was inspired by the French Revolution, which proved in no uncertain terms that liberty and equality were good, and rich people and privilege were bad. Wolfe Tone went to France to study revolution and his journal records him becoming more and more revolutionary with each *pain au chocolat* he consumed:

Took a walk by the Seine today with a *pain au chocolat* in my pocket … it seems clearer than ever that the connection with England must be severed and that when the chocolate doesn't go all the way from one end to another one's day cannot be salvaged.

Wolfe Tone, Journal, June 1791.

Revisionist Note #3:
It is often pointed out that many of Ireland's great nationalist heroes from history, such as Wolfe Tone, were Protestants. Nobody ever points out that many of England's great Nationalists, such as the Venerable Bede and Henrys I to VII were Catholics. This is a moderate oversight and historians should be mildly ashamed.

Ever since the French Revolution, the English establishment had been terrorised by French ideas which they feared would lead imminently to *fewer* stately homes and *more* ruffians with a say. When they heard Wolfe Tone had been to France thinking them, they decided to take several steps to abolish the threat.

One of these steps was to build Maynooth College so that Irish priests could be trained in Ireland instead of in Europe, where they were becoming infected with the contagion of French idées, and returning to spend the bit of Mass between the sermon and Communion reading Rousseau and building guillotines with their parishioners. The government also force-fed children brioche and made them watch street mimes until they began to claw desperately at the ground (usually within four minutes) and swore off anything French for life. This official paranoia was further reflected in an abuse of power that saw 368 people arrested for shrugging nonchalantly in Limerick alone, and a further 1,232 tried before a jury for playing *boules* (most were acquitted on the grounds that they were playing bowls).

Note:
Maynooth was also founded for a second reason: to appease the Catholic Church. This was one of many instances of the policy of 'conciliation' or 'appeasement' which the government turned to whenever they sensed upheaval. 'Conciliation' was often used in conjunction with, and immediately before, bouts of the government's other main policy: brutal repression.

Eventually Wolfe Tone came back to Ireland, slightly rounder and infinitely more revolutionised, and founded the aforementioned United Irishmen. The leaders were mainly professionals like lawyers, doctors and merchants, which proves conclusively that when they put their minds to it, middle-class people are capable of more than just building patios and putting money in savings accounts.

In 1798, the United Irishmen staged a rebellion. The 1798 Rebellion was the first Failed Rebellion of the Modern Era, or FROME I for short. The first stage of the rebellion took place mainly on Vinegar Hill and featured several of the following: priests, pikes, dreams of freedom; against several of the following: guns, cannons, armies.

At this stage the French agreed to get involved in Irish history and sent troops to Killala Bay in County Mayo. They went to the races at Castlebar to relax, then attacked the British forces and started marching towards Dublin. However, they were stopped and rousted by a large British faction in County Longford, which to this day is the most exciting fact about County Longford. The French then tried to land in Lough Swilly, with Wolfe Tone on board, but were discovered by a battalion of Royal Navy mackerel who surrounded the ship and captured it with the decisive efficiency that only a shoal of mackerel possesses.

Wolfe Tone was imprisoned but managed to execute himself before the English got a chance. This way, he died as a 'hero of the cause' and not a 'martyr to the cause'.

Test Your Knowledge:

1. Why was Vinegar Hill over there?

2. If Wolfe Tone had been called Fox Tone, Mono Tone, Póg mo Thóin, or Big Stone, would it have made him less heroic?

12

KINGDOMS UNITED

After FROME I, the British Government decided that the Irish absolutely categorically could not be trusted anymore. They decided that to keep a much closer eye on things, it would be altogether best if Ireland was brought right into the United Kingdom, instead of skulking outside like a hooligan waiting to throw a brick through the window.

Henceforth, Ireland was to have no parliament of her own and was to be governed directly from Westminster. This was the Act of Union of 1801 – a very important Act. Historians are often to be heard talking about Ireland 'under the Union', 'after the Union' and 'post-Union' which gives you some idea of how important it was.

The Act had to be passed by the Irish Parliament, which meant asking members to vote out of existence the Parliament where for years they had spent many enjoyable hours pretending to be important. An extensive campaign of bribery was therefore organised by Prime Minster Pitt the Toddler, who bestowed a plethora of titles and honours on Irish parliamentarians, including bishop, provost, raja, captain of industry, right halfback and treasurer, amongst others. Seventy-eight towns were invented in order to create mayoral and town crier positions, and numerous boards were established to generate chairman positions, such as the Ruminant Behaviour Board, and the Board for the Regulation of Postmasters General. One particularly unyielding MP, James Roughtrot Esq., made an impressive haul, becoming Mayor of Buncrana, Gorey and Dungarven; Bishop of Ferns and Ossory; Freeman of Tunbridge Wells, and Lady Captain of Kildare Golf Club.

Learning Exercise:
Think about the following for three minutes each: Acts, parliaments, unions. What have you *not* learned?

Not everybody in Ireland was happy with this new unified arrangement. One particularly angry individual was Robert Emmet. There are no likenesses of Robert Emmet from his lifetime, but as he was a young revolutionary who died after a glorious insurrection fighting the yoke of British imperialism, he was almost definitely very handsome and possibly had his shirt open a few buttons.

Emmet's rebellion was a disastrous failure, and so constitutes the second Failed Rebellion of the Modern Era or FROME II. The rebellion is memorable for producing Ireland's most nationalist housekeeper – Anne 'Nationalist' Devlin, who refused to give up her employer despite multiple threats of broom thrashings and several attempted linen whippings. The central role of housekeepers in Irish history is very much over-looked, although it is hoped that a soon-to-be published work, *Irish Housekeepers, 1200-Now: A History in 193 Volumes*, may go part of the way to filling this lacuna.

On the evening of 23 July 1803, Emmet marched in full military regalia to Dublin Castle, expecting to meet a 2,000-strong army of gallant insurgents wielding arms and shouting, 'Justice, Equality, etc.' under an ominous blood-red sky. Instead, he found three confused shopkeepers, five alcoholic children, several men who had drifted in from a laneway and a tearful dachshund who had lost his ball. Unsurprisingly, the rising was a failure.

During his trial, Emmet delivered one of Ireland's great-est ever speeches (see Appendix A), where he noted that his epitaph would only be written when Ireland took her place amongst the nations of the world, which most people agree happened in 1970, when a young girl from Derry sat on a stool and trilled the country to song-contest glory.

When the British Government was passing the Act of Union, the Prime Minister promised to grant Catholic Emancipation. He uttered this quietly under his breath, at the end of a speech about training more chimney sweeps, and later denied he had said it at all, but the people of Ireland definitely heard.

13

VERY LIBERATING

One of the people with the best hearing in Ireland was Daniel O'Connell. Of all those who felt betrayed by the British Government, Daniel O'Connell was the

most influential and by far the best dressed. He was a Catholic landlord and barrister, and – a little known fact – liked to relax by racing frogs down roads.

O'Connell came to be known as 'The Liberator' because he loved to liberate things, particularly people from oppression. He won Catholic Emancipation with help from Prime Minister Wellington, who gave his name to cowboy boots. This meant that Catholics who were voted into government could actually take their seats in Westminster, instead of sitting outside on stools.

Revisionist Note #4:
It was once a historical orthodoxy that all Catholic landlords were empathetic and grandfatherly and all Protestant landlords were callous brutes, but historians have uncovered evidence that undercuts this received wisdom. For instance, there was Fachtna O'Shanahan, a Catholic landlord from County Meath who took to riding tenants bareback around his estate as a form of weekend amusement. Meanwhile, Lord Twinkleton of County Louth was frequently seen handing out ducklings after Mass and every night he sang all the children on his estate to sleep. This kindly ritual took him up to seven hours to complete and children were often kept up until well past dawn, waiting for him to arrive on his lullaby rounds.

'The Harping of the Cattle'

See the vanquisher of the tyrant march,
With cape of emerald green,
And mop of patriot hair on his head,
To dear old Skibbereen.

The Liberator of the slave,
The harpist of the free,
The shattering of shackles shall yet sound,
From Celbridge to Ardee.

Thomas Moore (1830).

O'Connell went on to lead the campaign for the Repeal of the Union. He organised monster meetings, to which 8 million out of the 8 million inhabitants of the country travelled to hear him deliver rousing speeches, such as one at the Hill of Tara, from which the following extract is quoted:

> The onion of democracy has been peeled completely by the utensil of Catholic Emancipation. We, my dear fellow devoted peelers, must now REPEEL that onion with the utensil of hope and constitutional nationalism, etc., etc. Therefore, unite and REPEEL. The onion is mine and yours, etc.

Quite understandably, this metaphorical assault left many people bruised (metaphorically) and his campaign failed. Nonetheless,

Daniel O'Connell had proved that Irish people: (a) liked constitutional nationalism, and (b) struggled with metaphors.

Doubly confusing in all of this was the fact that the Prime Minister at the time was Robert Peel, leading many British people to suspect that O'Connell was in fact using an elaborate linguistic code to insult both the Prime Minister and edible bulbs.

This letter to the *London Outrage*, dated 5 June 1843, captures this concern:

Sir,

It has become abundantly clear that the arch-Hibernian, mop-haired demagogue in his rabble-rousing mania has enlisted a new weapon to his armoury: metaphoric outrage! The so-called O'Connellite Party are, it is shatteringly apparent, rampaging through the godforsaken countryside of their wild island lambasting our Prime Minister and threatening to do unto him such bulbous outrages as would shock the sensibilities of all who wear a waistcoat! All of this is undertaken in language shrouded in several shades of nightfall so as to render them impossible to understand to the unsuspecting, well-dressed gentleman. If our sister isle is ever to obtain the tranquillity which will enable it to be counted as a jewel in the belt of the uniform of the Empire, such manner of verbal *assassination* must be countered.

I am, yours, mine, truly, etc.

Mr Guffington, Esq., Guffington Hall, Essex.

Thus, the Irish Question was first posed. This was a notoriously difficult question to answer, particularly as nobody ever explained what it actually was; that there was a question at all was deemed to be enough.

Test Your Knowledge:

1. What is the icing on the cake of democracy?

2. Who was the cherry on top of the bun of Catholic Emancipation?

3. Did the cat of freedom arch its back and hiss at the neighbour's dog of religion?

14

BLIGHT AND CHILDREN

A vicious blight infected the potato crop between 1845 and 1850, which might not have been a problem except that almost everybody ate almost only potatoes almost all of the time. The British Government seemed disposed to help the starving masses at the beginning but after a while – forgetting that the Famine was not, in fact, a river – they decided it would be better to let it run its course. This is called '*laissez faire*' and it meant that about 1 million people died. The Famine also caused waves of emigration, which left deserted villages and evicted pigs.

Revisionist Note #5:
It is sometimes suggested that the British deliberately injected blight into each individual potato in Ireland. This is clearly ridiculous. In fact, they merely injected one potato in a field in Ahascragh without really thinking too much about it and it spread naturally from there.

It is often forgotten that the Famine also saw FROME III, in
the form of the Young Ireland Rebellion. The Young Irelanders
were a group of romantic, patriotic children who came together
during O'Connell's Repeel movement but left due to a lack
of crisps at Monster meetings, of which they were also fright-
ened. Their rebellion was an embarrassing failure, as most of
the rebels were under four foot tall and their guns were made
of wood painted in jolly colours. Nonetheless, Young Ireland
did bequeath a number of emblems which became integral
components of nationalist imagery and which, to this day, are
accepted symbols of the Irish nation, such as the harp, the shil-
lelagh, the Claddagh ring, the vomiting reveller, the 378-verse
ballad, and the shambolic queue.

In 1867, Ireland experienced FROME IV, the Fenian Rebellion. The Fenians were members of two Brotherhoods – the Fenian Brotherhood and the Irish Republican Brotherhood (IRB) – although ironically most of their membership was comprised of sisters from various religious orders. This prevalence of nuns has been overlooked by historians, who prefer to see nuns as pious and meek rather than the revolutionary firebrands the vast, vast majority actually are. This is a clear example of a minority being deliberately written out of history. Thankfully, a recent historiographical movement has begun to write nuns – along with similarly ignored groups such as *sous* chefs and trombonists – back into Irish history. The name Fenian was invented by the Irish in America, who later became Irish Americans, leading to the Kennedys and Massachusetts (although this is technically American history and therefore not interesting).

The IRB were committed to armed revolution as the only way to achieve an Irish Republic. This made them 'physical force Nationalists' as opposed to 'physically forced Nationalists', which is the term used to refer to Nationalists who required some vigorous shin kicking in order to ensure their commitment to the national cause.

Note:

The IRB was a secret society and as such formed part of a long and venerable tradition of secret oath-bound societies in Irish history. The Puck O'Turf Boys, for example, was a popular agrarian secret society of the 1780s who waged war on the fifty-eight Protestant bogs in the country. Such societies swore in members and organised innovative campaigns of intimidation, from upending cattle to setting squirrels loose on vicars, in order to upset the social order and protest against everything from tithes to clouds blocking the sun on days out.

The Fenian Rebellion was a complete fiasco due to poor planning and the fact that they had virtually no arms and precious few legs. The government had also made effective use of spies. Indeed, historians have since calculated that up to 85 per cent of Fenians were British spies. There were, in fact, only ever three real Fenians. They were executed in Manchester, becoming the Manchester Martyrs and reconfirming the symbolic importance of being executed by the British.

Learning Exercise:
Make a toy sword. Now do you see?

15

Ruling Home

The Home Rule Party was invented at this time to ask the Irish Question more loudly and in Parliament. It was led by Isaac Butt, possibly, but not actually, of Buttington Hall, Buttevant. Home Rule was a plea for an Irish Parliament which could control internal Irish affairs such as canals, Mullingar and the turnip harvest, while acknowledging that Ireland would remain part of the British Empire and cede control over matters such as defence, customs and proper freedom. As such, Home Rule was a form of limited self-government – a bit like being sent to the Gaeltacht or being a housewife in the 1950s.

One ingenious method the Home Rulers came up with for drawing attention to their cause was called 'obstructionism'. They would stand up in the Commons and deliver lengthy, pointless speeches about advancements in horse grooming and where they saw themselves in five years' time. One pioneering obstructionist, Joseph Biggar, once spoke for eight solid days on the exact age at which a woman becomes a spinster (twenty-eight).

Prime Minister William Ewart Gladstone believed he understood the Irish Question better than everyone else and thought the solution would be to introduce a law disembowelling the Church of Ireland in 1869. This was not, however, the correct answer.

Around this time, Michael Davitt arrived to ask the Irish Land Question. Historians are unsure as to whether this was a subset of, variant on, or accompaniment to the Irish Question. Meanwhile, Charles Stewart Parnell had appeared in Parliament to shout vigorously about Home Rule. Parnell, who had been head boy in school and was very neat, let his beard grow out and joined Davitt's gang of peasant radicals. This was the Land League. There followed an outbreak of boycotting and agrarian outrages: tenants boycotted rents; rents outraged landlords; landlords boycotted cattle, and cattle outraged polite society, as is their continual wont.

Gladstone, by now perplexed and vexed with Ireland, brought in somewhere between three and eighty-four Land Acts to stop all of this and answer the Questions. These Land Acts said:

- The land is important to the Irish.
- The Irish can take some of this land.
- The 3Fs.

Gladstone also put Parnell in Kilmainham Gaol to think about what he had done. After he came out, Parnell kept on asking the Irish Question, albeit more politely and with less hurling of turf at constables. The Land Question continued to be asked, however, and caused periodic outbreaks of Land Acts until eventually tenants were allowed to buy back the land with loans and landlords were forced to sell with reluctance.

In 1885, Gladstone and his Liberal Party agreed to support Home Rule and introduced a Home Rule Bill. However, many (one) of the Houses of Parliament disagreed, meaning Home Rule could not be passed into law. This is a pity, as it may have been the answer to the Irish Question, but we will never know. The Conservatives refused to support Home Rule and tried instead to kill it with kindness and cull it with compliments, baking lots of delicious Congested District Boards and telling Ireland it looked pretty on England's arm. Gladstone re-emerged a few years later to reintroduce Home Rule but again many (one) of the Houses of Parliament disagreed.

Note:

When they are feeling especially energetic, historians employ a technique known as a counter-factual. This means posing 'What if?' questions. For instance, 'What if Home Rule had been granted in the 1880s?'; 'What if the Easter Rising had taken place at Christmas in Alsace-Lorraine?'; 'What if Michael Collins had been born an uncle?', etc. Historians feel that by considering what *might* have happened, they will shed light on the relative importance of what *did* happen. Of course, this is nonsense, and a waste of time that might otherwise be profitably employed counting how many footnotes a colleague used, ranking other historians according to personal style, and arranging desk figurines in order of height. (For a glossary of other important terms see Appendix D.)

Like so many things in history, Parnell rose and fell. His fall was due to the love of a woman called Kitty O'Shea, whom the priests didn't like. As priests were 45 per cent of the population and controlled 74 per cent of the country's social mores, this meant he fell badly.

With Parnell gone, the Irish Question fell from the level of a question such as, 'What is the stars, what is the stars?' to the level of a question such as, 'Where is my sock, where is my sock?' Notwithstanding this, the Question continued to buzz around the cow's hide of the British political establishment, despite repeated attempts to swat it away with the tail of conciliation.

It should be noted here that it is often assumed that the British Government was consumed with the Irish Question. This is a grossly narcissistic assumption on the part of Irish people. In fact, Irish affairs were of piddling importance, and constituted only 4.2 per cent of teatime tittle tattle and 2.7 per cent of gin-swigging chin-wagging amongst the political establishment, who busied themselves with other pressing matters such as Boers, Dominions, Suez, etc.

Learning Exercise:
Imagine the Irish Question. What colour is it? What does it smell like? Is it rough or smooth? Does it have feelings like you and I?

16

MORE RULING HOME

It was around this time that Irish people started to become infinitely more Irish, thanks to organisations like the GAA, founded by Fr Michael Cusack, and the Gaelic League, founded by the Irish language. This was called 'cultural nationalism' or the 'Irish-Ireland movement' and it produced many poems and plays about Ireland as it was, as it is (*NB*: 'is' refers to 'now' back then and is therefore our 'was') and as it might yet be (*NB*: 'yet be' refers to the future back then, which may or not be our 'now').

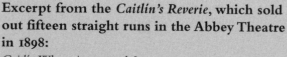

Excerpt from the *Caitlin's Reverie*, which sold out fifteen straight runs in the Abbey Theatre in 1898:

Caitlín: Where is me spade?

Widow O'Reilly: 'Tis in tha shed.

Caitlín: Thank ya, Missus.

James Óg (coming through the window): Will we race a donkey?

The Gaelic League taught people to speak Irish and love peasants, who were no longer seen as filthy pig ticklers and turf caressers but as pure, earthy manifestations of true Irishness. Daytrips from Dublin to view peasants in their natural habitats were organised by Lady Gregory, who was the most learned peasant spotter in Ireland and once shared a raw potato with a smallholder from Carlow. She vomited instantly to rapturous applause from Maud Gonne, etc. This, somehow, was part of the Literary Revival, which produced great culture and identity and some mild rioting over accents.

The GAA taught people to belt each other mercilessly with sticks on a pitch and charge half a day's wages for entry to under-twelve league semi-finals in the name of Éireann. Somewhat counterproductively, the GAA's focus on inculcating a crazed parish pride in fact rendered people useless to the

national cause, as they prided the local parish far, far above the nation. The priorities for most GAA players at the time ranked:

1. Parish
2. Jersey
3. County
4. Sausages
5. Ireland

While many people were getting more Irish, some people were getting infinitely less Irish. These people were called Unionists, and they said 'NO' in a League of Solemn Covenants signed in blood in 1912. Unionists feared that if Ireland was granted self-government they would be baptised Catholic in their sleep and forced to farm against their will. Fears also abounded that once Ireland achieved Home Rule, the Pope would move to Dublin, install himself on a throne on Grafton Street, and deliver edicts on the price of linen

Tensions mounted, as the Ulster Volunteer Force was set up and started running guns around Larne to give them some exercise. Not to be outdone, Nationalists set up the Irish Volunteer Force and, not wishing to appear ridiculous drilling with their mothers' discarded broom handles, also got some guns and ran these around Howth. The two forces also competed over who could jump highest (the UVF) and who could throw a boot the farthest (the IVF). They were both equally good at conkers.

Meanwhile, all the workers were locked out of work one winter due to Workers' Rights and Big Jim, while James Connolly threw a boot at a businessman but it missed. This was socialism, but it didn't last long.

Eventually, the First World War broke out due to European history, and the British Government put Home Rule on the shelf beside a jar labelled 'Burgeoning Indians'. Many Irish people joined the British Army to help win the war. These were mostly the same people who sat at the front of the class in school and always did their homework.

Test Your Knowledge:

1. Describe and explain the causes of Home Rule with reference to the following: clouds of independence, flares of governance, seas of disenchantment.

17

RISING NA CÁSCA

The people who sat at the back of the class and never did their homework organised the last Failed Rebellion of the Modern Era – FROME V – which was to become Ireland's most famous date in history. The 1916 Easter Rising took place in Dublin to the surprise of the people of Dublin. It began when Pádraig Pearse stood on the steps of the GPO and read out the Proclamation of Independence to a crowd of three puzzled amblers and eight confused strollers. The rebels then set up garrisons and waited to be bombed and shot at by British forces.

Pearse stood in a long tradition of romantic rebels who yearned for a free Ireland with the ardent passion of a young lover pressing his face up against his mistress's window until she starts crying and the police are called. He wrote many poems on the subject of revolutionary sacrifice and has often been compared with religious figures such as Poseidon and Thor. Pearse's Poseidon-like sacrifice has made him an object of commemoration, memorialisation, reconstruction and deconstruction, in a process known as 'creating an industry'.

The rebels were sorely lacking in weapons due to the failure of gunrunner Roger Casement to make a note of the right date in his diary. His recovered journal reveals that he had pencilled in 'tennis with Tim' over Easter weekend and 'Rising' the week after: an unfortunate lapse in personal organisation. The Rising was a complete failure and ended in a week.

However, when the British decided to execute the leaders, all was 'altered, altered completely: an appalling pulchritude was born,' in the words of William Yeats, butler to Lady Gregory. The rebels became Ireland's best ever martyrs to the cause.

From then on, people realised that Home Rule was both tedious and not going to happen. Everyone became ultra nationalist, leading to a countrywide surge in drilling, marching and saluting. Up and down the land, people were caught up in a frenzy of militarisation: marching to and from school and doctors' appointments, barking orders at each other in shops and attiring their children head to toe in khaki.

In 1918, there was a famous election where Sinn Féin won every single seat in Ireland, Wales, Scotland and the Isle of Man, as well as some seats in Luxembourg and Denmark. The newly elected MPs refused to take their seats in Westminster and instead set up a renegade parliament in Dublin, called the First Dáil. The British Government was unimpressed with this show of democratic impertinence and refused to acknowledge any of these goings-on, concentrating instead on leagues of nations.

18

FINE BIG LADS

Not long after this the War of Independence began. Columns of flying Republicans fought auxiliary Black and Tans under the leadership of Michael Collins, or 'The Fine Big Lad', as he was affectionately known. Collins set up a spy ring so extensive that eventually the entire British administration in Ireland, from Dublin Castle to Valentia lighthouse, was composed of Republican spies, who spied on each other to the point where everybody knew everything about everybody else expect that everybody else was a spy. Even Collins himself became confused by these labyrinthine subterfuges: at one point he worried that he wasn't even a Republican but rather Winston Churchill in disguise, until somebody pointed out that the latter would never have spent eight days hiding out as a schoolgirl in Terenure without having at least one cigar.

Collins was also a great military statistician, and eventually he brought the entire British Empire to its knees by reciting ratios of rifles to pistols *ad nauseum* and *as Gaeilge*. It was a great day, and Mother Ireland was proud of her sons and daughters. Collins went off to London to boast about winning and negotiate Irish independence. Much ink has been spilled by clumsy historians over the Treaty negotiations, and it has been pointed out that Collins and his team of clueless pinheads were no match for the sophisticated sophistry and agile argumentation of Lloyd George and Churchill. This ignores the fact that much of the negotiation was based on games of rounders and chess. Unfortunately, Collins and his clodhopper colleagues had heard of neither.

Collins came back with a Treaty creating the Free State, which he thought was the answer to the Irish Question. Lots of people, however, felt this was definitely the wrong answer, since it said that 68 per cent of Ireland was to be 72 per cent free, 88 per cent of the time.

The Treaty even included the following oath, which every Irish person had to say each morning in sombre tones while facing Buckingham Palace:

> I do solemnly swear true faith and allegiance to the Right Answer to the Question and that I will be faithful to His Majesty King George V, his children, children's children, children's children's heirs, etc., and admit that British people are slightly handsomer, their flag is nicer and St George is better than St Patrick, who probably had fat arms.

Irish people started fighting over the Treaty: those who favoured stepping stones across the river of conflict to the shore of freedom were FOR the Treaty; those who hated metaphors were AGAINST it.

Irregular and regular gorillas fought in the hills and bushes across Ireland. This was a very sad episode, as everyone had to fight their brother, or, if they didn't have one, their mother and aunts. The divisions were deep and to this day Irish people still resent their aunts slightly. In the end, the regulars won and the Free State was accepted by law as the answer to the Irish Question.

19

CAMÁN

The new Free State Government called itself Camán na nGaedheal, or 'hurl of the Irish'. Ireland was now a member of the Commonwealth of Patients, along with Canada, Tobago, etc., but could control many of its own affairs.

The Free State Government, intoxicated by these new powers (and possibly liquor), brought in over 400 Acts, including:

- The Intoxicating Liquor Act, 1925
- The Public Grooming Act, 1924
- The Most Things Stay the Same Act, 1923
- The Bunting Regulation Act, 1923

The Camán na nGaedheal Government was very conservative, hating change, progress, modernism, reform, etc. They kept all the old institutions the British had established, though they translated the names to Irish. The Garda Síochána were also set up around this time, to stop any residual brother–aunt conflict.

Above all, the new Free State Government loved draconian censorship. All films were censored except silent footage of Ireland's best First Holy Communions. All but seven books were banned, leaving public libraries stocked with little other than English–Irish dictionaries and copies of *Cooking with Sister Assumpta*. Cucumbers were heavily censored, and had to be dressed in little pants and jackets if on display in a grocer's window. The word 'censorship' itself was censored because it was deeply suggestive of things that might be censored.

Camán na nGaedheal also presided over the Boundary Commission, whose job it was to decide where exactly the Free State would end and Northern Ireland would start. In the end they left it how it was and this caused a severe outbreak of partitionism.

The economy at the time was heavily focused on agricultural exports, with Irish cattle supplying 78 per cent of British buffet beef. The greatest economic achievement was the establishment of the Electricity Supply Board and the construction of the hydro-electric station at Ardnacrusha on the Shannon, which enabled over twelve butchers in Carlow to light up plastic pig lights in their windows and allowed the Mayor of Roscrea to inaugurate the annual Roscrea Light Show, the three flickering bulbs of which drew crowds of thousands.

Eventually, however, Camán na nGaedheal thought it best to force another party into the Dáil, so that they could all argue about whether things were better now or not.

Test Your Knowledge:
1. Who was W.T. Cosgrave and why has he not been mentioned?

2. Describe and explain descriptions and explanations.

20

AMEN

men de Valera invented Fianna Fáil around this time, and made himself Taoiseach. He set about dismantling the Treaty bit by bit. Thus, he replaced the oath to the King with an oath to de Valera, for example. He also wore Irish dancing costumes to the Governor-General's annual ball and started an economic war with the British, during which an Irish cow won back the Treaty ports.

All of the above proved he was Ireland's best ever Nationalist. It was commonplace for Irish schools to display a picture of de Valera in the yard so that children could romp sturdily under his stern paternal gaze, and over 350 streets, housing estates and public buildings were promptly renamed in his honour, including De Valera Boulevard in Naas, De Valera View in Raheny and De Valera Lawn Tennis Club in Gorey.

In 1937, de Valera wrote a new Constitution with his friends the Irish Bishops. This said that Ireland was a great, holy nation and that Irish women were great mothers.

Excerpt from the 1937 Constitution:

Preamble: In the name of Holy Mary and Blessed St Joseph, we, the people of Éire, in remembrance of the independent blood of our rampaging ancestors and in recognition of the glorious blood-stained struggle for Freedom, seeking to take our place amongst the glory of Free independent nations as Free sons and Free daughters of the Fianna, do hereby enact this Constitution.

Article 1.1: Ireland is a full island with all the counties.

Article 1.2: Ireland is a very holy island and the Church is very special, i.e. dominance of society, culture, morals, education, hairstyles, weekly shop.

Article 1.3: Irish women are the best mothers and this should be celebrated by letting them be mothers and little but mothers until they die as grandmothers.

Amen had an Emergency during the Second World War and had everyone neutered just in case. In Northern Ireland, by contrast, nobody was neutered and after the war they had welfare and prosperity. Amen told everyone not to think about the North; this stopped people from feeling jealous and learning about standards of living. Various measures were taken to enforce this policy. North was removed from all compasses and was disallowed as a direction, while only a South Pole appeared in geography books. All of this rendered the Irish very poor at mapmaking and to this day Ireland has not produced a single champion cartographer.

Important Revisionist Note #6:

De Valera's 1948 St Patrick's Day speech is commonly misquoted, making him seem like a backward-looking bumpkin-idoliser. In fact, he did not refer to 'comely' maidens or 'dancing at the crossroads' at all.

What he actually conjured up was 'a land whose countryside would be bright with cosy homesteads, whose fields and villages would be joyous with the sounds of industry, with the romping of sturdy children, the contest of athletic youths and the laughter of happy maidens'.

As you can see, this in no way describes a romanticised rural idyll at odds with anything approaching societal progress.

21

OTHER PARTIES

After between forty-two and sixty-two years in power, the people got tired of Amen and Fianna Fáil, and elected some other parties. These were the inter-party governments and they were comprised of every party that wasn't Fianna Fáil.

By this stage, Camán na nGaedheal had dyed its shirts blue and changed its name to Fine Gael. While Fine Gael and the other parties represented disparate and often opposing political ideals, they were united by exasperation with the length of Fianna Fáil's term in office. This is called a coalition government and it happens regularly to this day.

Learning Exercise:

1. See if you can spot the pattern in Irish Government succession:

Fianna Fáil, Other Frustrated Parties, Fianna Fáil, Other Frustrated Parties, Fianna Fáil …

During the First Inter-Party Government, Ireland decided it was well enough to leave the Commonwealth of Patients and so declared to everyone that it was now a Republic and therefore 29 per cent more Free than when it was a Free State. It still lacked Northern Ireland, but this fact was mostly forgotten about anyway, due to not looking at it for fear of catching standards of living, sterling, shipyards, etc.

At this time in Ireland, medical treatment focused on the dispensing of rosary beads and the sprinkling holy water. All this was set to change when Dr Noel Browne, the only Irish doctor who was not also a parish priest, suggested a plan to treat mothers and children using stethoscopes, medicine and hospitals. This was called the 'Mother and Child Scheme'. The Catholic Church objected to this attempt to undermine its supreme mastery of all and so cancelled the First Inter-Party Government.

Indeed, the Catholic Church had scaled to the summit of its powers during the 1940s and '50s, mostly thanks to Archbishop John Charles McQuaid, who was not only Emperor of the Catholic Church but also sat on thirty-eight government committees, managed the GAA and the postal service, controlled the water supply, and ran a shoe shop. McQuaid, like most of the clergy at the time, hated progress, subordination

and socialism, and loved praying, episcopal conferences and pointing out sins.

Here is a table of what was considered a sin and not a sin in 1950s' Ireland:

A Sin	Not a Sin
Dancing	Walking Quietly
Opinions	The Angelus
Buttocks	Soda Bread
Protestants	Jumpers

The Church also contributed to the extremely high rate of emigration at the time, with one particularly gloomy Mass leading to the departure of the majority of population. This was 'Mass emigration' and some commentators predicted the disappearance of the entire population, barring a light smattering of prelates and a few stubborn Presentation nuns. The lack of women and preponderance of bachelors in the country at this time led to a decrease in children, mirth and personal grooming. Some of these bachelors returned to school, just to give teachers somebody to teach. This resulted in a generation of adults who knew the times tables up to 12 x 13, further than any generation in history.

The Second Inter-Party Government followed shortly after but it achieved so little that no historian has ever written anything about it. This is called 'glossing over' and it is an acceptable historical methodology when dealing uninteresting periods.

As a result of the above, nobody has as yet bothered to count how long the Second Inter-Party Government remained in power, but sooner or later people began to hanker after Fianna Fáil, as this was by now the established pattern. They were duly elected back into power, although Amen decided to retire as he was now 285 years old and had held every office in the state twice.

22

SEÁN THE MASS

Seán Lemass, the new Fianna Fáil overlord, was of Huguenot descent. Lemass (or 'The Mass' in English) decided Ireland needed to look outward and so he bought everybody in the country a television set and started importing swimming togs, restaurants and bananas. Having bought everybody a television, he felt it best to put a channel on that television. He therefore invented Telefís Éireann, which broadcast one and a half hours of Irish dancing every night from 1961 to 1968. Families would stand in front of the television and dance along with the broadcast, leading, over time, to weakened living-room floors and national excellence in dance.

Learning Exercise:
Draw a political map from de Valera to Lemass and include various features of the landscape, including hills of modernity and seas of economic self-sufficiency.

T.K. Whitaker drew up the First Programme for Making the Economy Happen in Ireland, which set out various steps by which the country might start creating an economy. Ireland's first industrial estate was built in Shannon, County Clare, to start the industrial revolution of which Ireland had previously been so suspicious, due to its being English and not farming. The remains of at least three industries have been excavated at the Shannon site, including a vast doorbell factory and an apparent attempt at a steel works, which most likely floundered in the face of a debilitating shortage of the key component of steel (i.e. buns).

The doors of the economy flew open to let in the stiff breeze of foreign investment, whilst allowing the cooking smells of exports to waft out. Eventually, in this way, the economy started to happen. There was a new sense of hope as people considered staying in the country for the first time in over a century.

New and radical ideas flooded into Ireland, leading directly to short skirts and Gay Byrne. This was called social change and it occasioned a deep questioning of the dominance of the Church and showbands. These latter had enjoyed a stranglehold of unbridled power over the music industry. For decades, Irish people had been battered over the heads, metaphorically and actually, by tyrannical acts like Jimmy Bop and the Archbishops and Big Mick and the Shovels. Young people were herded against their will into parish halls by priests wielding sticks every Saturday night and forced to perform terrified jives until 11 p.m.

In the Northern Irish Parliament, Lord Basil Byron Baldrick Beaverbrooke was replaced by Terence O'Neill, who believed in Catholics and held meetings with Lemass on the subject.

This led directly to a cacophony of Ian Paisley over the coming decades. There was huge tension in the North of Ireland as to whether, and how, Catholics might be allowed to exist (e.g. not at all, quietly, in poverty, over there, with hats on) and what role the government in the South of Ireland might play in the six counties they didn't own but said they did, but probably wished they didn't.

23

GRACE AND PAISLEY

Warning:
The next few chapters cover a period of history which is quite close to the period of Right Now, where history ends for the time being. This relative lack of perspective makes it difficult to determine what is important history and what is not important history. For instance, is it more important that the 1970s witnessed the unstoppable rise of Brendan Grace or Ireland's joining of the European Economic Community? It is virtually impossible to tell from this short distance.

In the 1970s, a young Dublin comedian named Brendan Grace leapfrogged from the showband circuit to mainstream comedy success, garnering an average of 5.6 hearty chuckles per minute during live shows. His rise to fame is reflective of very important things, as this cultural historian points out:

Brendan Grace was the essence of the post-colonial moment in
Ireland, encapsulating as he did the conflict in the public sphere
between the *representation* of what it *symbolises* to *mean* to be Irish
on the one hand and a fat man in a schoolboy outfit on the other.
This was the birth of the moment that *made* Twink in the womb
of Brendan's possibility, in order to *unmake* de Valera, who becomes
the archetypal 'spinster aunt moment' in Irish history.

*Mashing the colonial potato: Encountering the female Paddy in post-
history Ireland* (1998).

Note:
Academic historians, despite their many, many, many
virtues and charms, are admittedly prone to giving somewhat grandiose titles to their works. Thus it is always
important to read the subtitle and contents page of a history book. For instance, one history book with the title
Ireland, Economy and Commerce in the Nineteenth Century
had the subtitle (written in font size 4) *A Study of the
Basket-weaving Trade in East County Clare, 1814-1817*. Chap-
ter titles included, 'Making the baskets: the story of Sheila
Dowd's basket, 1 July 1815' and 'The market economy: the
basket stall on market day in Lisdoonvarna'.

Also in the 1970s, Ireland held the third of approximately 781
constitutional referenda when it voted to join the EEC/EC/
EU. It did this in an attempt to become more European and
therefore more sophisticated and stylish. The Europeans gave
the famers some nice new CAPs to spruce them up, which

made everyone intensely jealous as farmers were traditionally the least stylish and previously their headwear had been made from discarded copies of the *Clare Champion*. Other things Europe gave us were: equality (e.g. you cannot be fired for being from Offaly), a working knowledge of French ('*Ou est les bons bons?*'; '*La plage*', etc.) and a desire to establish industrial triangles.

Feminism happened at about this time too, leading to Mary Robinson and fewer children. Married women, who had previously been banned from paid employment in case they forgot to make dinner, were allowed back into the workforce. Overall, this caused career women and eventually, after a long struggle, Anne Doyle.

In 1969, serious Trouble broke out in Northern Ireland, caused by Gerry Mander and civil rights. This was initially part of the '60s and democracy and protest, but it soon became part of terrorists and killing. About this time, the 'N' was reinstated as part of the Irish compass, as it was now important to look North, whether people wanted to or not.

The Sunny Day Agreement tried to get everybody to share the power but it failed due to 'NO'. Ian Paisley, in a moment of quiet reflection explained this:

NO to the cursed ABOMINATION of governments out to destroy last BASTION of God-fearing Protestant GLORY in Ulster. NO, we will not allow priests and holy communion children to ride ROUGHSHOD around our province. NO, we will not bow in subjection to the TRAITOROUS filthy lying British Government. NO, we will not allow the Republic to roll around in our affairs like so many pigs in a pen, with their filthy LYING ABOMIABLE TREACHEROUS ways desecrating the pure God-fearing right of Ulster Protestants to never SURRENDER!

Ian Paisley, Speech to the pupils of St Winifred's Primary School, Ballymena, 1979.

24

SLIGHTLY BETTER

With things getting out of hand, Good Garrett the Taoiseach signed the Anglo-Irish Agreement with Thatcher Thatcher Milk Teeth Snatcher (so called because she allegedly wrenched teeth from children's heads to relax). This also failed to solve the Trouble (it was described by Ian Paisley as an 'ABOMINATION'), which overshadowed the good things that happened during this period, such as Knock Airport and Barry McGuigan.

Occasionally, Fianna Fáil were out of power due to some inevitable coalitions, but these usually gave Fianna Fáil some excuse to return to power sooner rather than later. For example, when the coalition led by Good Garret tried to tax children's shoes it was removed from office. This demonstrates the power of the children's lobby in Ireland, an often despotic interest group that to this day have a stranglehold on the price of stickers and Fanta. Since then, governments seeking to raise funds have instead focused on taxing the old, infirm and lowest paid.

Around this time, Fianna Fáil produced one of its most famous leaders. This was Charles Jehovah Haughey. In the 1980s, during a particularly bad recession, he reminded everyone to tighten their belts in what turned out to be Ireland's worst ever speech. Charles J. mislaid his own belt and taxes, and therefore bought an island, a mansion and a yacht filled with shirts.

This was also a period of intense industrial unrest. On average, people went on strike once every 2.5 weeks. April 1982 saw all-out strikes by teachers, bus conductors, butchers, calligraphers and window shoppers. It is a wonder that the country managed to function. But it is a good thing it did, because things were starting to get better in some ways.

The Peace Process broke out in the 1990s when people realised nobody would win. Mary McAleese, Ireland's second most important woman after Mary Robinson (who got there first), was elected President in 1997. As a Catholic from Belfast who read the Book of Common Prayer and took Holy Communion in synagogues, people felt she represented the way forward. Gerry Adams had his voice turned back on by the BBC and Ian Paisley became widely viewed as a Protestant Santa figure.

Culturally, this period was dominated like a wrestler astride a donkey by U2 and their frontman Bono, who once declared Ireland to be 'like a Jewish Palestine, yeah, yeah, yeah,' during an eighty-minute monologue between songs. Other cultural highlights included Bob Geldof ending hunger, 'Crazy World' by Aslan, and Derek Davis's annual Christmas Day speech, which in 1989 ran for four solid hours and included three instances of unwarranted nudity and four warranted.

It was in 1990 that Ireland achieved what was undoubtedly its crowning achievement as a nation, when Dave O'Leary kicked a ball with his foot past a man into a net. This put Ireland into the quarter finals of the World Cup sports competition against Italy, meaning we had achieved everything, and so we all sold up our belongings and went to Italy to live out the rest of Irish history there. After we lost that match the entire country returned, bankrupt but not unhappy, a bit like the feeling of sunburn in the evening.

Test Your Knowledge:
1. Is Bono an existential nightmare?

25

BOOM!

The Boom was the most recent, officially designated, period of Irish history. Indeed, it was designated as a distinct historical period while it was actually happening, with people at the time regularly making pronouncements such as 'This week during the Boom I ate ham, Andy', and posing questions like, 'Is your mother enjoying the Boom this weather, Andy?' The Boom was also commonly referred to as the Celtic Tiger in an effort to enable metaphors involving the word 'roaring'.

One of the earliest indicators that Ireland was about to become a rapidly expanding economy based on rampant free-market deregulation and house-of-sand wealth creation was a breathtaking series of wins at the Eurovision Song Contest, which hinted at the level of socio-political debasement to which the nation was willing to submit itself.

American multinationals flocked to Ireland, attracted by tax incentives and a well-educated workforce with nice accents. By the 1990s, approximately 83 per cent of companies trading out of Ireland were American. Also about this time, property started borrowing from cheap banks, they both went into a tent with the government, and the country became very rich.

In this new Ireland, people routinely drank coffee from crystal slippers on their way to work. Children attached chandeliers to their schoolbags and wiped their faces with Pucci scarves during P.E. Most people owned three or four houses, which they rented to each other or to themselves. It was not uncommon for somebody to buy a house in the morning and sell it on to themselves by lunchtime for 11 per cent more. Bacon and potatoes were replaced by braised squid and caramelised onions as the staple diet of the country. Memberships

to exclusive gyms soared, along with obesity, in a paradox known as the 'Rich Fatty's Guilt'. A chain of restaurants opened which served meals in martini glasses on tables made of bent over tramps.

Some pointed out that not everybody was getting their share of the wealth; others warned that things couldn't continue as they were. However, all of these people they were drowned out by the sound of the head of the Central Bank driving an electric golf caddie around the building screaming, 'Pancetta and rubies for all!'

This was also a period of tribunals, which took place to decide just how corrupt on a scale of 'Jesus' to 'Fianna Fáil' various people were. Most of these people were in Fianna Fáil.

Test Your Knowledge:
1. How much champagne did the average Irish child quaff between 1995 and 2003?

26

RIGHT NOW

During the period of Right Now, Ireland is in a very bad recession. The country has received some rather large loans and is being overseen by a troika of organisations who are insisting that Ireland learn some restraint after her enthusiastic, if unseemly, binge. As such, Ireland is more akin to a performing seal, clapping for fish, than a functioning economy. Leading the clap is Taoiseach Enda Kenny, who is either a steady hand steering the ship of state through choppy waters or a robo-conservative manufactured in Munich, programmed by technocrats and set to 'unalarming'.

Certainly, the country is currently unwell. The Ward Sisters in Fine Gael and Labour have proven very good at taking blood, but it is unclear if they have any disinfectant to sanitise the ward and protect it from outside infection.

However, we won't get into this here as it is not quite yet history, being as it is, still continuing. Irish history therefore ends at this point here.

EPILOGUE

And so, Ireland's long and winding history flows through the valley of time and into the ocean of the future. Some say that history is a guide to the future, prophesising tomorrow and stomping the rain dance that will water the crops of posterity. For this reason, historians are often asked onto television to explain *then* and *now* and *tomorrow*, giving them a range of knowledge unsurpassed by any other type of swot.

Using the historical knowledge we have gained from the preceding chapters, it is therefore possible to say with ferocious certainty that:

1. In 2016, the Pope will ride through the Phoenix Park on a donkey.

2. The Guinness factory will close and reopen as Ireland's first velodrome, finally meeting the disregarded needs of Ireland's 721 cycling enthusiasts.

3. Mayo will become a principality in 2020.

4. In the 2036 war between Belgium and Holland, we will finally be forced to abandon our neutrality and fight alongside our brave Dutch comrades.

With such certainties afoot, you may ask whether there is any point reading the newspaper anymore, or campaigning for a velodrome in Mullingar? And here it is possible to admit that history doesn't always signpost us in exactly the right direction. Sometimes it offers us raincoats just before the sun comes out or sets out a picnic by the river only for the heavens to open. Sometimes it sings us lullabies when we should be waking up and at other times again it shouts in our ears when all we need is some quiet.

Indeed, you might argue, if history teaches us anything, it is that nothing is as certain or important as the fact of you, sitting in your seat, right now, reading this word here.

Appendix A

Ireland's Top Five Speeches

1. Robert Emmet's trial speech, 1803
Strong points: passionate, eloquent, tore open his shirt halfway through.
Weak points: spinach in teeth.

2. De Valera's, St Patrick's Day speech, 1943
Strong points: multiple references to romping.
Weak points: overemphasis on firesides.

3. Enda Kenny's 'It's not your fault' speech, December 2011
Strong points: absolved nation of sin of economic crash.
Weak points: failed to give anyone penance, forgot his cassock, Jamaican accent.

4. Queen Elizabeth II's speech, May 2011

Strong points: sorry for everything, all friends now.

Weak points: section on holiday in Crete unnecessary.

5. Daniel O'Connell's Hill of Tara speech, 1843

Strong points: audience of 8.3 million, hair looked nice.

Weak points: only 0.000002 per cent of the audience could hear him.

Appendix B

Components of Irish History

Components of Irish History

Appendix C

Change in Irish Society

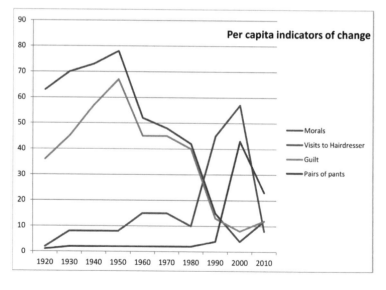

Appendix D

Glossary of Other Important Terms

Archaeologist: hairy demi-person who squats and digs in mud for bits of old saucepan, which they then label and put in bags.

Historian: attractive, charming individual who gathers evidence about the past and very generously shares with others what she or he has learned in the interest of furthering our collective human knowledge for its own sake.

Comparative history: drawing comparisons and contrasts between different places. Like having a twin, comparative history suggests that you may not be special and mother's favourite after all.

Historical orthodoxy: the received wisdom of the ages that is always right, e.g. de Valera had glasses; the Celts were fiery and warlike; Birr, County Offaly, once offered the position of mayor to a donkey, who turned it down on the spot.

Methodology: the principles and rules historians follow in reconstructing the past. Usually set out in one to three sentences at the start of a book.

Oral history: listening to people's accounts of the past over biscuits and trying to figure out the extent to which they are embellishing, lying or confusing their lives with something they saw on television.

Revisionism: the process of ruining the party by turning up sober, switching off the music, and asking, 'Who's going to clean up this mess and why is the cat in the dryer?'

Appendix E

Appendices

Appendices are where scholars put information that is too unimportant or too tedious to include in the main body of the text. They are usually determined to include this material, however, as it proves they are hard working. Appendices are often the most derided parts of books and are overlooked by the vast majority of readers. This cruel neglect is a shame; one study has found that over 3 per cent of appendices are mildly informative.

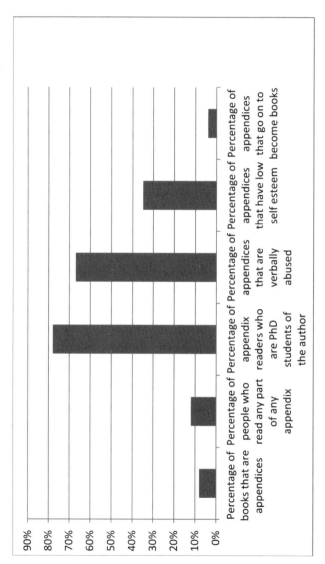

Snip's

Psalms 139